Motor Racing at
Brands Hatch
in the seventies

Chas Parker

To Ollie,

Best Wishes,

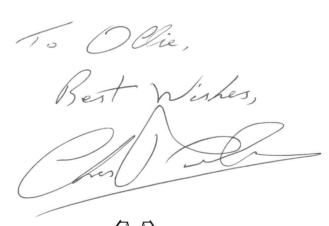

VELOCE PUBLISHING
THE PUBLISHER OF FINE AUTOMOTIVE BOOKS

Also from Veloce Publishing

SpeedPro Series
4-Cylinder Engine - How to Blueprint & Build a Short Block for High Performance by Des Hammill
Alfa Romeo Twin Cam Engines - How to Power Tune by Jim Kartalamakis
BMC 998cc A-Series Engine - How to Power Tune by Des Hammill
BMC/Rover 1275cc A-Series Engines - How to Power Tune by Des Hammill
Camshafts - How to Choose & Time them for Maximum Power by Des Hammill
Cylinder Heads - How to Build, Modify & Power Tune Updated & Revised Edition by Peter Burgess
Distributor-type Ignition Systems - How to Build & Power Tune by Des Hammill
Fast Road Car - How to Plan and Build New Edition by Daniel Stapleton
Ford SOHC 'Pinto' & Sierra Cosworth DOHC Engines - How to Power Tune Updated & Enlarged Edition
by Des Hammill
Ford V8 - How to Power Tune Small Block Engines by Des Hammill
Harley-Davidson Evolution Engines - How to Build & Power Tune by Des Hammill
Holley Carburetors - How to Build & Power Tune by Des Hammill
Jaguar XK Engines - How to Power Tune by Des Hammill
MG Midget & Austin-Healey Sprite - How to Power Tune Updated Edition by Daniel Stapleton
MGB 4-Cylinder Engine - How to Power Tune by Peter Burgess
MGB - How to Give your MGB V8 Power Updated & Revised Edition by Roger Williams
MGB, MGC & MGB V8 - How to Improve by Roger Williams
Mini Engines - How to Power Tune on a Small Budget 2nd Edition by Des Hammill
Motorsport - Getting Started in by S S Collins
Rover V8 Engines - How to Power Tune by Des Hammill
Sportscar/Kitcar Suspension & Brakes - How to Build & Modify Enlarged & Updated 2nd Edition by Des Hammill
SU Carburettors - How to Build & Modify for High Performance by Des Hammill
Tiger Avon Sportscar - How to Build Your Own Updated & Revised 2nd Edition by Jim Dudley
TR2, 3 & TR4 - How to Improve by Roger Williams
TR5, 250 & TR6 - How to Improve by Roger Williams
V8 Engine - How to Build a Short Block for High Performance by Des Hammill
Volkswagen Beetle Suspension, Brakes & Chassis - How to Modify for High Performance by James Hale
Volkswagen Bus Suspension, Brakes & Chassis - How to Modify for High Performance by James Hale
Weber DCOE, & Dellorto DHLA Carburetors - How to Build & Power Tune 3rd Edition by Des Hammill

Those were the days ... Series
Austerity Motoring by Malcolm Bobbitt
Brighton National Speed Trials by Tony Gardiner
British Police Cars by Nick Walker
Crystal Palace by Sam Collins
Dune Buggy Phenomenon by James Hale
Motor Racing at Brands Hatch in the Seventies by Chas Parker
Motor Racing at Goodwood in the Sixties by Tony Gardiner
Three Wheelers by Malcolm Bobbitt

Enthusiast's Restoration Manual Series
Citroen 2CV, How to Restore by Lindsay Porter
Classic Car Bodywork, How to Restore by Martin Thaddeus
How to Paint Classic Cars by Martin Thaddeus
Triumph TR2/3/3A, How to Restore by Roger Williams
Triumph TR4/4A, How to Restore by Roger Williams
Triumph TR5/250 & 6, How to Restore by Roger Williams
Triumph TR7/8 How to Restore by Roger Williams
Volkswagen Beetle, How to Restore by Jim Tyler

Essential Buyer's Guide Series
Alfa GT Buyer's Guide by Keith Booker
E-Type Buyer's Guide
Porsche 928 Buyer's Guide by David Hemmings
VW Beetle Buyer's Guide by Richard Copping

General
1950s Motorsport in colour by Martyn Wainright
AC Two-litre Saloons & Buckland Sportscars by Leo Archibald
Alfa Romeo Berlinas (Saloons/Sedans) by John Tipler
Alfa Romeo Giulia Coupe GT & GTA by John Tipler
Anatomy of the Works Minis by Brian Moylan
Armstrong-Siddeley by Bill Smith
Autodrome by Sam Collins
Automotive A-Z, Lane's Dictionary of Automotive Terms by Keith Lane
Automotive Mascots by David Kay & Lynda Springate
Bentley Continental, Corniche and Azure by Martin Bennett
BMW 5-Series by Marc Cranswick
BMW Z-Cars by James Taylor
British 250cc Racing Motorcycles by Chris Pereira
British Cars, The Complete Catalogue of, 1895-1975 by Culshaw & Horrobin
Bugatti Type 40 by Barrie Price
Bugatti 46/50 Updated Edition by Barrie Price
Bugatti 57 2nd Edition by Barrie Price
Caravans, The Illustrated History 1919-1959 by Andı Jenkinson

Caravans, The Illustrated History from 1960 by Andrew Jenkinson
Chrysler 300 - America's Most Powerful Car 2nd Edition by Robert Ackerson
Citroen DS by Malcolm Bobbitt
Cobra - The Real Thing! by Trevor Legate
Cortina - Ford's Bestseller by Graham Robson
Coventry Climax Racing Engines by Des Hammill
Daimler SP250 'Dart' by Brian Long
Datsun 240, 260 & 280Z by Brian Long
Dune Buggy Files by James Hale
Dune Buggy Handbook by James Hale
Fiat & Abarth by Andrea & David Sparrow
Fiat & Abarth 124 Spider & Coup by John Tipler
Fiat & Abarth 500 & 600 2nd edition by Malcolm Bobbitt
Ford F100/F150 Pick-up 1948-1996 by Robert Ackerson
Ford F150 1997-2005 by Robert Ackerson
Ford GT40 by Trevor Legate
Ford Model Y by Sam Roberts
Funky Mopeds by Richard Skelton
Jaguar MkII by Andrea & David Sparrow
Jaguar, the Rise of by Barrie Price
Jaguar XJ-S by Brian Long
Karmann-Ghia Coup & Convertible by Malcolm Bobbitt
Lambretta Ll by Andrea & David Sparrow
Land Rover, The Half-Ton Military by Mark Cook
Lea-Francis Story, The by Barrie Price
Lexus Story, The by Brian Long
Lola - The Illustrated History (1957-1977) by John Starkey
Lola - All The Sports Racing & Single-Seater Racing Cars 1978-1997 by John Starkey
Lola T70 - The Racing History & Individual Chassis Record 3rd Edition by John Starkey
Lotus 49 by Michael Oliver
Mazda MX-5/Miata 1.6 Enthusiast's Workshop Manual by Rod Grainger & Pete Shoemark
Mazda MX-5/Miata 1.8 Enthusiast's Workshop Manual by Rod Grainger & Pete Shoemark
Mazda MX-5 (& Eunos Roadster) - The World's Favourite Sportscar by Brian Long
Mazda MX-5 Miata Roadster by Brian Long
MGA by John Price Williams
MGB & MGB GT - Expert Guide (Auto-Doc Series) by Roger Williams
Micro Caravans by Andrew Jenkinson
Mini Cooper - The Real Thing! by John Tipler
Mitsubishi Lancer Evo by Brian Long
Morgan Drivers Who's Who - 2nd International Edition by Dani Carew
Motorhomes, The Illustrated History by Andrew Jenkinson
Motor Racing Reflections by Anthony Carter
MR2 - Toyota's Mid-engined Sports Car by Brian Long
Nissan 300ZX & 350Z - The Z-Car Story by Brian Long
Pass the Driving Test
Pontiac Firebird by Marc Cranswick
Porsche 356 by Brian Long
Porsche 911 Carrera by Tony Corlett
Porsche 911R, RS & RSR, 4th Edition by John Starkey
Porsche 911 - The Definitive History 1963-1971 by Brian Long
Porsche 911 - The Definitive History 1971-1977 by Brian Long
Porsche 911 - The Definitive History 1977-1987 by Brian Long
Porsche 911 - The Definitive History 1987-1997 by Brian Long
Porsche 911 - The Definitive History 1997 on by Brian Long
Porsche 914 & 914-6 by Brian Long
Porsche 924 by Brian Long
Porsche 944 by Brian Long
Porsche Boxster by Brian Long
Rolls-Royce Silver Shadow/Bentley T Series Corniche & Camargue Revised & Enlarged Edition by Malcolm Bobbitt
Rolls-Royce Silver Spirit, Silver Spur & Bentley Mulsanne 2nd Edition by Malcolm Bobbitt
Rolls-Royce Silver Wraith, Dawn & Cloud/Bentley MkVI, R & S Series by Martyn Nutland
RX-7 - Mazda's Rotary Engine Sportscar Updated & Revised New Edition by Brian Long
Singer Story: Cars, Commercial Vehicles, Bicycles & Motorcycles by Kevin Atkinson
Subaru Impreza by Brian Long
Taxi! The Story of the 'London' Taxicab by Malcolm Bobbitt
Triumph Motorcycles & the Meriden Factory by Hughie Hancox
Triumph Speed Twin & Thunderbird Bible by Harry Woolridge
Triumph Tiger Cub Bible by Mike Estall
Triumph TR6 by William Kimberley
Triumph Trophy Bible by Harry Woolridge
Turner's Triumphs, Edward Turner & his Triumph Motorcycles by Jeff Clew
Velocette Motorcycles - MSS to Thruxton Updated & Revised Edition by Rod Burris
Volkswagen Bus or Van to Camper, How to convert by Lindsay Porter
Volkswagens of the World by Simon Glen
VW Beetle Cabriolet by Malcolm Bobbitt
VW Beetle - The Car of the 20th Century by Richard Copping
VW Bus, Camper, Van, Pickup by Malcolm Bobbitt
Works Rally Mechanic by Brian Moylan

First published in 2004 by Veloce Publishing Limited, 33 Trinity Street, Dorchester DT1 1TT, England. Fax 01305 268864/e-mail info@veloce.co.uk/web www.veloce.co.uk or www.velocebooks.com
ISBN 1-904788-06-8/UPC 36847-00306-7
Readers with ideas for automotive books, or books on other transport or related hobby subjects, are invited to write to the editorial director of Veloce Publishing at the above address.
British Library Cataloguing in Publication Data - A catalogue record for this book is available from the British Library. Typesetting, design and page make-up all by Veloce Publishing Ltd on Apple Mac. Printed in Italy.

Contents

Dedication

To Jonathan and William, for keeping the interest alive.

Acknowledgements

Thanks to: Chris Dobson for giving me all those old issues of *Autosport*, Bob Reid for letting me keep them in his garage – I knew they would come in useful one day, and Alan Hall, who was a regular companion at the races for so many years, and whose reminiscences helped jog my memory over a pint or three.

Brands Hatch programmes and passes from the author's collection: reproduced with permission from the British Racing and Sports Car Club and the British Automobile Racing Club. All photographs are the author's own.

Bibliography

Sundry copies of *Autosport* from 1970–79; *Motor Racing Year 1973*, ddited by John Blunsden. Published by Motor Racing Publications 1973; *From Brands Hatch to Indianapolis*, by Tommaso Tommasi. Published by Hamlyn 1974; *25 Years of Brands Hatch Car Racing*, by Mike Kettlewell. Published by Brands Hatch Circuit Ltd. 1975; *Motor Racing Year 1977*, edited by John Blunsden. Published by Motor Racing Publications 1977; *Brands t Bexhill*, by Max Le Grand. Published by Bookmarque Publishing 1995; www.etracksonline.co.uk

Foreword

My first experience of Brands Hatch was at a club meeting on a freezing December day in 1969. It snowed, my older sister complained, and the wind howled through the canvas back of the grandstand at the entrance to Paddock Hill bend. My main recollection, apart from the inclement weather, is that the grids were mainly made up of Minis and Austin Healeys.

My second visit was more memorable, although the weather was just as unpleasant. It was April 1970 and the World Championship sports cars were paying their annual visit to the circuit for the BOAC 1000. This was magical, pure heaven, except that the heavens opened for a closer look, shedding torrential rain.

I had caught a Maidstone & District coach to the circuit from Bexhill and, when we arrived, I stepped off into a very large puddle. I looked around to find the quickest route out of the water but there wasn't one; the puddle seemed to extend as far as I could see in each direction. It was raining very, very hard and within a couple of minutes I was very, very wet. Being young I viewed rain as an inconvenience rather than a potential cause of pneumonia, and so I trotted off in the knowledge that I was already as wet as it was possible to get and that there was little point worrying about it. I spent the next six-and-three-quarter hours - that was how long the race lasted - walking round and round, getting to know every inch of Brands Hatch like the back of my hand.

Signs were different in those days; I found one next to the bridge over Pilgrim's Drop, on the long part of the circuit, with a large arrow pointing back the way I had come. It read: 'Toilets, Refreshments and Druids.' The latter, I assumed, being on sale with a premium charged for High Priests ...

After that visit I was hooked, and spent many weekends over the next decade standing up at Druids Hill hairpin, my favourite spot, watching a feast of motorsport.

Under the direction of John Webb the circuit thrived throughout the seventies. Webb had a reputation for being careful with money that led to a memorable piece of graffiti in the toilets: 'In the interests of economy, patrons are requested to use both sides of the paper, signed John Webb.'

Brands Hatch may not have been the most luxurious place in the world, and the facilities and the hamburgers (or swampburgers as a friend aptly referred to them) could be particularly nasty at times, but it had a friendly feel and the racing was always good. What made it stand out was the viewing; the short circuit sat in a natural amphitheatre so that, from almost any point, you could see virtually the whole way round. The first time I went to Silverstone I was hugely disappointed at having such a limited view, the circuit being on an old airfield and the whole track lying quite flat. Brands, as far as I was concerned, was simply the best motor racing circuit in the world.

From the start-finish line on Top Straight, the circuit plunged steeply downhill at the right-hand Paddock Hill bend, and then climbed quickly up Pilgrim's Rise to the sharp right hairpin at Druids. From there it was downhill again to the left-hand Bottom Bend, along the misnamed Bottom Straight, which curved gently to the left behind the pits, and then the left-hander known as Kidney Corner (but not featured as such on any maps). There the track divided. The 1.24 mile long Club circuit turned quickly right again into the long, sweeping Clearways corner which took you back on to Top Straight, while the 2.65 mile Grand Prix circuit continued left around Kidney and out into the country. A long, gently climbing straight took the cars under a bridge before plunging downhill at Pilgrim's Drop and then up Hawthorn Hill into the fast, uphill, right-hander of Hawthorn Bend.

into the fast, uphill, right-hander of Hawthorn Bend. The short Portobello Straight took them into another right-hander, Westfield, before the track dropped again into Dingle Dell where it kinked right and climbed up into yet another right-hander, Dingle Dell Corner. From there it was a short blast down to the tight, and slightly cambered, left-hander of Stirling's Bend which led on to a long straight taking the cars to the lengthy sweep of Clearways, and on to Top Straight. A challenging track. A driver's track. A spectator's track.

Introduction

It's sometimes hard to believe that the gently sweeping bowl in the Kent countryside, which was to become one of the most famous motor racing circuits in the world, started life as a mushroom field belonging to the nearby Brands Hatch Farm.

Its potential was first noticed by a group of cyclists in 1926; they thought that the natural amphitheatre would make a splendid cycle track. The farmer gave his permission, and over the next few years the field became a popular venue for both bike and motorcycle enthusiasts, with a three-quarter mile circuit laid out for grass track racing. During the war the area was used as a vehicle park by the military, but afterwards the motorcycles returned and, in 1947, Brands Hatch Stadium Ltd was formed.

In 1949 it was decided that a permanent circuit should be established to allow both motorcycle and car racing. Over the winter of 1949-50 a one mile asphalt track was laid and, on 16 April, 1950, the first car race, for 500cc Formula Three cars, took place and 10,000 spectators turned up.

The circuit was kidney-shaped and the cars ran anti-clockwise. It wasn't until 1954 that they started running clockwise, which they have done ever since. In the winter of 1953 the loop up to Druids was added, extending the track length to 1.24 miles. In 1955 the first permanent grandstand was built, and the following year a telephone link was installed between race control and all the marshals' posts. During the winter of 1959 the Grand Prix loop was added, and the first race on the 2.65 mile track, for Formula One cars, took place on August Bank Holiday 1960, and was won by Jim Clark.

Early in 1961 Grovewood Securities acquired a controlling interest in Brands Hatch which, by now, was established as a world-class circuit, and a man named John Webb joined the board of directors. Webb had been asked by Brands MD John Hall to find a large company to help develop the track. At the time Webb worked for a London PR company, Brands Hatch being one of his clients. He approached Grovewood, a property and investment company, which saw the potential to develop the circuit. Webb was installed as Executive Director and, over successive years, Grovewood also acquired Mallory Park, Snetterton, and Oulton Park. A new company, Motor Circuit Developments (MCD), was formed in 1966, headed up by Webb.

Meanwhile, improvements were made to the circuit with a new startline control tower, new restaurants, toilet blocks, and lock-up workshops all being added. The British Grand Prix was held at the track for the first time in 1964 and given the honorary title of Grand Prix of Europe - a new paddock bar and the Grovewood Suite being built in time for it. In addition, an illuminated scoreboard was erected at the exit of Clearways, and a number of shops opened behind the main grandstand.

Over the next few years the circuit flourished under the direction and imagination of Webb. The Race of Champions, for F1 cars, was first held in 1965, and in 1967 Formula Ford was introduced as an 'under £1000' formula. In 1969 Webb and Nick Syrett, then Executive Director of the British Racing and Sports Car Club (BRSCC), came up with Formula 5000 as a big power, low cost formula, which proved a hit with spectators. And so the circuit headed into the seventies, which is where I came in ...

1970

By 1970, Brands Hatch was already established as one of the major motor racing circuits in the world, and the BOAC 1000 kilometres (or 500 miles as it had been until that year) for World Championship sports cars was already regarded as something of a classic. The 1970 season was set for a battle between the two sports car giants of the time, Porsche and Ferrari. Those were the days when Formula One drivers regularly raced in endurance events as well as Grands Prix, and spectators thrilled to the sight of Jacky Ickx, Denny Hulme, Jack Brabham, Jo Siffert, and Piers Courage battling in these 4.5 litre monsters.

The race has gone down in motor sport history for the performance by the Mexican driver Pedro Rodriguez in the John Wyer Automotive Engineering Gulf Porsche 917. The rain that day was torrential, and Rodriguez put on what was described in one report as a 'virtuoso display of wet-weather driving that has rarely been matched'.

It was all the more remarkable because he had been called into the pits after only a few laps for a dressing-down by the clerk of the course for passing under the yellow flag while debris on Top Straight was being cleared up. After this Rodriguez drove as though he were oblivious to the conditions, passing cars with apparent ease. He out-braked Chris Amon's Ferrari 512S at Paddock, and then, coming out of Clearways, pulled alongside Vic Elford in another 917 and into a lead he was never to relinquish. He stayed at the wheel for the maximum three-and-a-half hours permitted before handing over to co-driver Leo Kinnunen. By this time the rain had stopped, but the track was still far from dry.

After a short spell at the wheel, Kinnunen, totally outclassed on this day by his team mate, handed back to Rodriguez for the remainder of the race. At a quarter to seven that evening Rodriguez took the chequered flag, five laps ahead of the second placed Vic Elford/Denny Hulme car. I remember seeing the two winners at the prize-giving after the race. A slight figure, Rodriguez looked almost mischievous, with an impish grin on his face. It was obvious that he had thoroughly enjoyed himself.

The Swiss driver Jo Siffert in one of the most beautiful racing cars ever made, the John Wyer Automotive Engineering Gulf-Porsche 917, in the 1970 BOAC 1000. The race was memorable for the mesmeric drive of Siffert's team mate, Pedro Rodriguez, who won the race by five laps in appalling conditions. Sadly, Siffert lost his life at the circuit the following year.

My next visit to the circuit was on a bright, sunny day in May for FordSport Speed Day. This was a club meeting, enhanced by the presence of a number of Grand Prix drivers such as Jackie Stewart, Graham Hill, Piers Courage, and John Surtees, who were there to compete in a race for identical Ford Capri 3000s. The meeting, as the name suggests, was sponsored by Ford and, if you drove a Ford car, admission was free. Jackie Stewart gave a demonstration run in his Formula

One March-Ford 701, there were displays of Fords and Ford-powered vehicles, rides round the circuit in Transit vans, and Chris Barber's jazz band was on hand to entertain the crowd.

In July, I attended my first ever British Grand Prix. Jochen Rindt, in the beautiful, Gold Leaf-sponsored, Lotus-Ford 72 was my hero, and on pole position alongside Jack Brabham's Brabham-Ford BT33, and Jacky Ickx in the 312B Ferrari. Ickx led away but after only six laps the Ferrari's differential gave up. Brabham and Rindt battled throughout the race and, with just a handful of laps left, it looked like victory was going to go to the Australian.

One lap to go and the two cars crossed the line, Brabham quite a way ahead of Rindt, who appeared to have settled for second, but a lap later it was Rindt who came into sight first, Brabham limping slowly round the last corner having run out of fuel. I was elated; my first Grand Prix and the right man had won.

I attended two major race meetings at the track that year, and both proved memorable - no wonder I had developed a liking for the place.

One of the Chevron-Ford B16s of the 'up-to-2-litre' class in the 1970 BOAC 1000. This car was entered by Worcestershire Racing Association and driven by John Burton and Mike Walker. It retired after 101 laps with fuel pump and ignition problems.

The BOAC 1000 kilometre race catered for the same World Championship Sports Cars that ran at the famous Le Mans 24 Hours.

It's May 1970, and FordSport Speed Day. The Formula F100 race has just started, and the crowd watches expectantly as the field heads towards Paddock Bend. Ray Allen, in his Royale, led from start to finish. Formula F100 was new that year and was intended to be a sports car version of Formula Ford. It was named after the Firestone tyre used in the category but was not a success, and was abandoned after just two seasons.

A feature of FordSport Day was the BEA Trident Trophy race for identical Ford Capri 3000GTs, featuring drivers such as reigning World Champion Jackie Stewart, Graham Hill, John Surtees, and eventual winner Piers Courage. Here, the cars are lined up on the grid, prior to the start.

At the end of the meeting, Jackie Stewart was to be found in the paddock, having lost the keys to his car! Earlier he had run demonstration laps in his Formula One March-Ford 701.

1971

I visited Brands only once during 1971, and that was for the BOAC 1000. The previous year's event had left such an impression on me that it was unthinkable to miss it. Also, it was to be the final year that the magnificent 917 Porsches and 512 Ferraris would be running, a change in the regulations limiting engine size to just three litres.

The race was to throw up a surprise result. Ferrari, anticipating the change in regulations, had entered a single three litre 312P model for Jacky Ickx and Clay Regazonni, the intention being to develop it in readiness for the following season. The car qualified on pole but lost time after hitting a back marker, running trouble free, thereafter, to second place. The Porsches failed to deliver, and it was left to the three litre Alfa Romeo T33/3 of Andrea de Adamich and Henri Pescarolo to take the marque's greatest win since the 1950s, albeit somewhat unexpectedly.

Ferrari, not having enjoyed the success it had hoped for with its 512S and 512M models, decided to use the '71 season to prepare for the coming of the 3 litre category in 1972. Its 312P model, with Jacky Ickx and Clay Regazzoni at the wheel, proved quick and reliable. The car led the race initially but was delayed by an accident early on and eventually finished second.

Rolf Stommelen and Toine Hezemans co-drove this Alfa Romeo T33/3 in the 1971 BOAC 1000, and led until the engine blew with little more than an hour to run. Fortunately for Alfa Romeo the pair's team mates, Henri Pescarolo and Andrea de Adamich, took the victory.

Before that, back in March, the Race of Champions provided a popular victory for Clay Regazzoni in the Ferrari 312B-71. The race saw the debut of the first ever gas turbine-powered Formula One car, the Pratt & Whitney-engined Lotus 56B, driven by Emerson Fittipaldi. The car retired with broken suspension.

The other major international event which took place at the circuit that year was the Victory Race on 24 October, intended to be a celebration of Jackie Stewart's second Formula One World Championship. Instead, it turned into tragedy and highlighted a number of shortcomings regarding the safety of the track.

On lap fifteen Jo Siffert's Yardley-BRM P160 came down under the bridge at Pilgrim's Drop, into Hawthorn Bend, and swerved left, right, and left again, hitting the bank and bursting into flames, killing its driver.

Highlights of the race were shown that same afternoon on television, and I can still picture the pall of smoke rising above Hawthorn Bend, visible all over the track. Raymond Baxter, who was commentating, gave an emotional account of the tragedy and the programme closed with him looking into the camera, tears running down his cheeks.

The subsequent inquest heard that three of the fire extinguishers at the nearest marshals' post were not working properly, and that Siffert died from asphyxia due to the fire. His only injury was a broken left leg. A verdict of accidental death was returned with the rider that there could be 'better supervision of safety and fire precautions'. While it was agreed that firefighting methods could be improved, it was also thought that they would be too costly and impractical to implement. An accident like this was simply accepted as part and parcel of racing.

This was the last year we would see the all-conquering 5 litre Porsche 917s as the Championship would run for 3 litre cars the following year. Here, the Pedro Rodriguez/Jackie Oliver JWAE 917 rounds Druids Bend.

1972

Over the winter a number of safety improvements were made at the track, including the installation of hundreds of wooden sleepers facing the protective banks around most of the circuit. The Armco guard rail was also extended, as was the run-off area at certain points, and spectator viewing areas were improved.

Uncertainty hung over Brands Hatch during the early part of the year, as the proposed route of the new M20 motorway looked as if it would encroach on the existing paddock area, and there was a threat that the circuit might have to close for the duration of the construction work. The route was only one of several being considered, but uncertainty over the plans meant that the much needed new pits, paddock, and tunnel between the two, originally intended to be constructed in time for the Grand Prix, would not be ready.

Emerson Fittipaldi gave notice of the Formula One season ahead when he convincingly won March's Race of Champions in his JPS Lotus-Ford 72, beating Mike Hailwood in a Surtees-Ford TS9B, and Denny Hulme's McLaren-Ford M19A.

Derek Bell takes the Gulf Mirage M6 up Hailwood Hill towards Druids in the 1972 BOAC 1000. This was to be the last time the event was held, although other long-distance sports car events did take place at the Kent circuit.

The Ferrari mechanics jump on board the victorious Ferrari 312P-72 of Jacky Ickx and Mario Andretti, who led home team mates Tim Schenken and Ronnie Peterson for a Ferrari 1-2. The third car, of Clay Regazzoni and Brian Redman, finished fifth.

A month later and it was BOAC 1000 time again and my annual pilgrimage to see the long-distance sports cars. The race provided a walkover for the Ferrari team, its cars finishing one-two with victory going to the pairing of Jacky Ickx and Mario Andretti.

There were fun and games at FordSport Day in May, with Grand Prix drivers such as Emerson Fittipaldi, Graham Hill, and François Cevert racing in identical black Ford Capris.

The idea of providing something different to entertain the crowds continued at the British Grand Prix in July, sponsored this year by John Player, and given the title Grand Prix of Europe, to honour the 75th anniversary of the RAC. Twenty-five competitors (mainly F3 drivers) took part in the 'Tour de Hatch' - a one-lap bicycle race around the short circuit.

The British Grand Prix, which alternated between Brands Hatch and Silverstone, was held on a Saturday despite most others being on Sundays. Entry cost £2, plus £2.50 for a grandstand seat. Practice on Thursday

It's FordSport Day again and this is Cyd Williams in a March 722A in the Formula Atlantic race. Formula Atlantic was introduced in 1971 along the lines of Formula B in the USA to provide 'Formula Two on the cheap' and was for single-seater cars using 200hp engines of up to 1600cc, based on production units. Williams, who had started from the front row, finished fourth, having been black-flagged for overtaking under the yellow and called into the pits for a dressing-down.

The American driver Bill Gubelmann in a Formula Atlantic March 722. Gublemann dived into Paddock Bend in the lead on the first lap and stayed there throughout, despite the best efforts of Cyd Williams.

1972 was the year of Ferrari domination in the World Sports Car Championship. Having been developed during the previous season the 312P-72 3 litre sports prototype was unbeatable, winning every race it entered. Here, Clay Regazzoni leads team mate and eventual winner, Jacky Ickx, through Paddock Hill bend.

Motor Racing at Brands Hatch in the seventies

Formula One paddocks were completely accessible in those days. This is the Brabham-Ford BT37 of Carlos Reutemann at the 1972 British Grand Prix. Reutemann finished in eighth place after being delayed by a collision with Carlos Pace's March-Ford 711.

Chris Amon's fourth-placed Matra Simca MS120C is closely inspected by one of the younger spectators at the event. Amon had passed Hulme for fifth place on lap 68 of the 76-lap race and inherited fourth when the March of Ronnie Peterson crashed at Paddock, two laps from the end.

The BT37 of Reutemann's team mate Wilson Fittipaldi is loaded onto the Brabham transporter at the end of the day. The Brazilian was classified twelfth but was not running at the finish.

Niki Lauda's STP March-Ford 721G sits in the paddock. The Austrian finished ninth.

and Friday attracted 16,000 spectators with 50,000 on race day.

The race provided a three-way fight between Jacky Ickx in the Ferrari 312B2, Jackie Stewart in the Tyrrell-Ford 003, and Emerson Fittipaldi's JPS Lotus-Ford 72. Ickx led until lap forty-nine, when he retired with an oil leak, handing the lead to Fittipaldi. Stewart had hounded the Brazilian, getting past him at one point, but Fittipaldi regained the position and took a clear victory.

Just over a month later, on August Bank Holiday weekend, the track hosted what was billed as 'the richest race in Europe'. The Rothmans 50,000, so named because of its £50,000 prize fund, was open to all-comers and the hope was that it would attract F1, F2, F5000, Indycars, sports cars, and Can Am competitors. It was to be held over 118 laps of the Grand Prix circuit, with a first place prize of £10,000.

Up to 100 cars were expected to enter but, even just a month before the event, the entries were completely unknown, although most F1 teams - except Ferrari and Matra - were expected, as was at least one current Can Am car.

It wasn't to be. Spectator attendance was poor, with some people deeming the £2 entry fee too high, while date clashes with Can Am and USAC races in the States, and an Interserie round in Finland, kept away the Indy, Can Am, and big-engined sports cars. Meanwhile, having fought against a proposal to introduce pit stops in F1 in 1973, the Grand Prix teams were hardly in a position to compete in a long-distance race. They would have had to either modify their cars by adding larger fuel tanks, which the few who entered did, or not turn up. In the event, it turned out to be a third victory at the track for Fittipaldi, driving a JPS Lotus-Ford 72.

There was also a poor turnout for the end-of-season John Player Victory Meeting, though bad weather was a contributory factor to a crowd of just 15,000. The race produced a surprise result with Jean-Pierre Beltoise in the Marlboro-BRM P180 taking the win from Carlos Pace and Andrea de Adamich's Surtees-Ford TS9Bs.

The Rothmans 50,000, held on the August Bank Holiday weekend, was intended to be the biggest Formula Libre event ever. It was hoped that a mix of Formula One, Formula Two, Indycars, sports cars, and Can-Am machinery would compete for 'Europe's richest-ever motor race'. Cars which failed to qualify for the main race competed in a 100 kilometre 'sprint' earlier in the day. Here, Bob Wollek drives the 2 litre Chevron-Ford B21.

Henri Pescarolo in the Frank Williams March-Ford 711, and Howden Ganley in the Marlboro BRM P160C, with extra side fuel tanks and a high-mounted wing, on the run up to Druids on the formation lap of the Rothmans 50,000. Pescarolo finished third while Ganley retired on lap 47.

Following his win at the British Grand Prix the previous month, Emerson Fittipaldi in the JPS Lotus-Ford 72 came home an easy winner of the Rothmans 50,000. The car sported an extra three-gallon fuel tank mounted behind the roll-over bar for it to be able to complete the race distance.

David Purley, driving the Lec Refrigeration-sponsored Formula One March-Ford 721G, alongside Carlos Reutemann in the Formula Two Rondel Racing Brabham-Ford BT38. Reutemann's car is fitted with pontoons on each side to carry extra fuel. Neither car finished the race.

FordSport Speed Day included a race for Grand Prix drivers in identical Ford Capris.

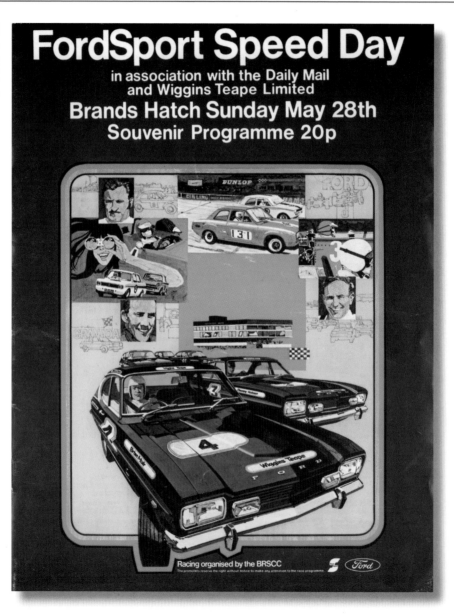

1973

It was overcast and cold for the annual Race of Champions in March, but the rain held off and a crowd of 45,000 saw an unexpected victory for Peter Gethin's F5000 Chevron beating the more fancied F1 runners.

Jean-Pierre Beltoise in a Marlboro BRM P160E led away from Ronnie Peterson's JPS Lotus-Ford 72, and Niki Lauda in another BRM. After seven laps John Watson crashed his Brabham-Ford BT42, breaking his right leg in two places. Lauda pitted on lap 16 for new rear tyres, and Peterson's gearbox gave out after eighteen laps. Beltoise was now leading but his tyres were also deteriorating, so he pitted on lap 22, re-joining sixth. After twenty-five laps Mike Hailwood's Surtees-Ford TS14 led from Denny Hulme's McLaren-Ford M23, Vern Schuppan (BRM), Peter Gethin (F5000 Chevron-Chevrolet B24), and James Hunt, making his F1 race debut, in the Hesketh Surtees-Ford TS9B.

Schuppan slid off on lap 36, and Hailwood crashed at Hawthorns, so Hulme took over as the fourth leader of the race. With only a handful of laps to run he slowed as his clutch began to give up, and Gethin took the lead with two laps left, Hunt only just failing to pip Hulme for second.

Motor Circuit Developments' initiatives to draw more people into race meetings, such as having famous sporting personalities in a celebrity event at the Race of Champions, seemed to be working. In May a race was held for radio DJs in identical ShellSport Escorts

McLaren's new challenger for the 1973 season - the Gordon Coppuck-designed M23 - had made its race debut in South Africa, where Denny Hulme had led. Hulme gave the car its European debut at the Race of Champions, taking the lead five laps from the end, but losing it again with just two to go, eventually finishing second.

The Race of Champions, held in March each year, was the curtain-raiser to the European Formula One season. Here, the supporting Formula Atlantic race gets under way with Tom Pryce (34) in the Royale trying to out-drag Cyd Williams (15) in the Brabham who has rocketed off the fourth row. Eventual winner Colin Vandervell (7) in a March, and Stan Matthews (Ensign) follow. Note the mass of spectator cars on South Bank. It was a Brands tradition for all the cars there to sound their horns in recognition of each race winner as they went round on their lap of honour.

- a certain Noel Edmonds won comfortably and announced that he wouldn't mind doing a bit more racing in the future. The DJ versus record company race ensured that the grandstands were filled despite atrocious weather.

Some 11,000 people then turned up in August for the Sutton & Cheam Motor Club-organised Radio Luxembourg Day, which included a 'host of personalities from the pop music world'. Luxembourg's tie-in turned a club meeting, which would have normally attracted 1500 to 2000 people, into a much larger event.

BMW organised a day as well, which included demonstrations, parades, parachute jumps, and a House of Commons versus House of Lords race (won by the Earl of Denbigh). Around 8000 turned up, many attending for the first time, and a *TV Times* Race of the Stars meeting in October attracted 10,000 spectators.

Formula 5000 was the main attraction at the customary end-of-season international meeting, October's Motor Show 200, the category enjoying its

The three Marlboro-BRM P160s of Jean-Pierre Beltoise, Niki Lauda, and Vern Schuppan lead the field away at the start of the Race of Champions on a grey March afternoon. Behind them are the fast-starting JPS Lotus-Ford 72s of Ronnie Peterson and Emerson Fittipaldi, and the McLaren-Ford M19 of a young Jody Scheckter. Eventual winner Peter Gethin, in a Formula 5000 Chevron, is back on the fourth row.

The race saw the Formula One debut of James Hunt, driving the Hesketh-entered Surtees-Ford TS9B. Hunt acquitted himself well, finishing third behind Gethin and Hulme.

best season since its inception five years previously. It was the final round of the Rothmans European F5000 championship and four drivers could still take the title - Teddy Pilette, Tony Dean, Steve Thompson, and Tom Belso. Clay Regazzoni, having only his second F5000 outing in the Jones-Eisart Lola T330, was an added bonus for the European championship as the car usually only ran in the American series.

Guy Edwards, in his Lola-Chevrolet T330, took a gamble on using special tyres brought to the meeting by Goodyear and it paid off, the conditions suiting them perfectly. He started tenth, but moved rapidly through the field and took the lead on lap 31, holding it until the end, while Teddy Pilette secured the title.

As the fuel crisis began to hit the country, MCD announced in November that all race meetings at Brands Hatch would be cut back by twenty per cent in race distance and, by the end of the year, motor sport faced an uncertain future. Petrol was rationed and it was unlikely that racing could restart in 1974 if these restrictions stayed in place. As a result, the traditional Boxing Day meeting at the circuit was cancelled.

Despite the uncertainty, MCD announced plans for a major refurbishment, costing £50,000. This included a

If it's May it must be FordSport Day: a gaggle of Ford Escort Mexicos stream down from Druids and around Bottom Bend on the first lap.

Eventual winner Donald MacLeod (1) in a Merlyn and Derek Lawrence (Dulon) dispute the lead of the British Oxygen Golden Helmet Formula Ford Race.

Motor Racing at Brands Hatch in the seventies

Formula Atlantic races were a staple diet of meetings such as FordSport Day and provided close and exciting racing. Colin Vandervell in the Triplex March-Ford 73B is just holding off David Purley in the older Lec-sponsored 722 model. The positions were reversed at the flag. The pair remained only a few feet apart for the majority of the race.

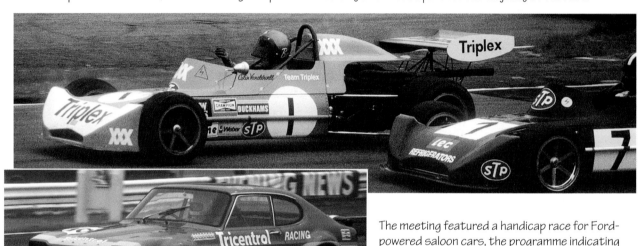

The meeting featured a handicap race for Ford-powered saloon cars, the programme indicating that 'any modifications allowed provided shape of cars remains as original'. This is 'scratchman' Mick Hill driving the 4.7 litre Ford Boss Capri V8 in which he set fastest lap. Hill made up ground rapidly but spun at Paddock on lap 8.

August Bank Holiday Monday at Brands, and the forerunners of today's British Touring Car Championship provided spectacular racing in those days, too. The Championship was run for International Group Two saloon cars and one of the front-runners was Brian Muir, in the Dealer Team BMW 3.0 CSL. The car was dubbed 'the Batmobile' because of the image created by its front spoiler and rear aerofoil. Unfortunately, it retired on the sixth lap when the oil pump seized.

Up at Druids, Frank Gardner powers the brutish 7 litre Camaro past the smaller class Escort GT of Oli Thatcher, on his way to both winning the race and establishing the lap record for the short circuit for Group 2 saloons.

Australian Frank Gardner, in the SCA Chevrolet Camaro, and Brian Muir in the BMW 3.0 CSL, lead the field around Paddock Bend at the start of the *Evening News* Touring Car Trophy Race. On this occasion it was Gardner who emerged the victor after Muir retired.

new 550-seater grandstand opposite the pits and 1600 terraced seats. The pit lane was to be widened, and ten new pit buildings added. Spectator earth banks at Paddock and Clearways were to be pressure-seeded to become grassy banks, and, most importantly from the spectator's point of view, new toilets were to be built.

A full re-siting of the main paddock could not begin until work on the new M20 motorway had started, however. The route of the motorway would pass through car parks a short distance from the existing paddock, but racing would be able to continue. Because of the modifications to the circuit, it would be closed throughout January and the first half of February 1974.

The different classes in the Touring Car Championship meant that the massive 7 litre Camaros ran against the likes of this 1300cc Mini Cooper S, driven by Richard Ellice.

Gijs van Lennep powers his ShellSport Luxembourg
Lola-Chevrolet T330 around Druids at the August Bank
Holiday meeting. He finished ninth.

One of the stalwarts of the F5000 series was the Belgian
driver Teddy Pilette. This was to be his day, taking the VDS
Chevrolet-powered Chevron B24 to victory from Tom Belso's
ShellSport Luxembourg Lola T330.

Guy Edwards was known as the master of the sponsorship
deal, managing to entice a number of high profile names
into the sport during the seventies. On this occasion his
Barclays-backed Lola-Chevrolet T330 finished sixth.

Peter Gethin, a master of Formula 5000, won the
Championship in 1969 and 1970. His Chevron B24 retired
due to engine problems on the 58th lap whilst leading
comfortably and having set fastest lap.

The main race of the day on August Bank Holiday Monday was the round of the Rothmans European Formula 5000 Championship, which drew large crowds. Peter Gethin, winner earlier in the year of the mixed F1/F5000 Race of Champions, leads the field up Hailwood Hill towards Druids.

The popularity of the sport drew high profile sponsors such as Shell and Radio Luxembourg.

Motor Racing at Brands Hatch in the seventies

Another of the circuit's regular meetings was the Motor Show 200, held in October each year. One of the featured races in 1973 was the final round of the John Player Formula Three championship, which provided a well-deserved win for young Tony Brise in the *Kent Messenger* March 733, here in the middle of the 3-2-3 grid at the start of the race. Flanking Brise are Ian Taylor and Michel Leclere.

Ian Ashley, in the Henley Forklift F5000 Lola T330, waits in the collecting area in the paddock. After battling for the lead he picked up a puncture, pitted for a new rear tyre, and promptly spun off at Paddock Bend.

In the paddock sits the Hexagon Racing Trojan-Chevrolet T101 of John Watson, who finished third in the main event of the day.

The spoils of victory. Tony Brise's team celebrates after he convincingly won the John Player Formula Three event and took the Championship title with it.

1974

At the beginning of the year Motor Circuit Developments announced what it called 'the greatest programme of events in the history of Brands Hatch'. The jewel in the crown was, of course, the John Player British Grand Prix to be held in July. The other Formula One event on the calendar was the Race of Champions, while World Championship sports cars were due to return after a year's absence for the British Airways 1000 in September. Also on the programme were Rothmans F5000 Championship races to be held on Easter Monday, August Bank Holiday, and at the October Motor Show 200 meeting. Interspersed between these were a couple of Radio One and Radio Luxembourg meetings, BMW and FordSport Days, and the usual varied championship and club meetings.

This year's Race of Champions meeting was very wet, as seen in this shot of John Nicholson in his Formula Atlantic Lyncar-Ford. Nicholson finished in fifth place.

The 1974 Race of Champions saw the UK debut of the new Hesketh-Ford with James Hunt at the wheel. Hunt was out of luck, despite qualifying on pole position he spun on the second lap in the atrocious conditions, and then tangled with a back marker before retiring.

The event went down in history as the race where Belgian Jacky Ickx took the lead from Niki Lauda's Ferrari on the outside of Paddock Bend in the wet. Here, Ickx's JPS Lotus-Ford 72 battles for second place with the Texaco-Marlboro McLaren-Ford M23 of Emerson Fittipaldi, who finished third.

A crowd of 41,000 turned out for the Race of Champions in unpleasantly wet conditions. The race attracted a healthy entry of sixteen F1 cars and was augmented, as usual, by the F5000 runners. James Hunt, the new hero of the day, was on pole in the Hesketh-Ford 308 but spun at Druids on the second lap. The race is remembered for Jacky Ickx, in the sole JPS Lotus-Ford 72, overtaking Niki Lauda's Ferrari 312B3 around the outside of Paddock Bend to take the lead a few laps from the end.

A group of friends and I travelled up the evening before the British Grand Prix, spent some time drinking at the Portobello Inn on the A20, and then camped in the car park. We were in the circuit by six in the morning and found a spot at the top of Druids. In the days before catch-fencing and run-off areas, you were close to the

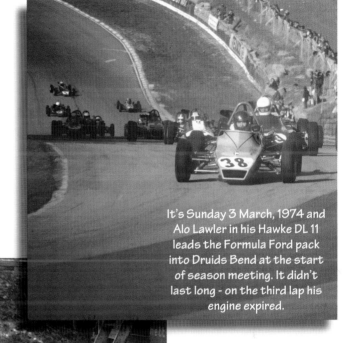

It's Sunday 3 March, 1974 and Alo Lawler in his Hawke DL 11 leads the Formula Ford pack into Druids Bend at the start of season meeting. It didn't last long - on the third lap his engine expired.

Easter Monday and it must be F5000 again. Mike Wilds' immaculate Dempster March-Chevrolet 74A sits in the paddock prior to the main event of the day. It was Wilds' first full season of F5000 and yet he was leading the Championship at this point. He claimed pole position for the race but dropped to sixth by the finish after suffering brake problems.

cars - you didn't need a long lens to take good photos - and it all added to the atmosphere and the excitement.

The racing that day was excellent; from the Formula Atlantic event, won by future World Champion Alan Jones, to the *Evening News* Showbiz Challenge for the ShellSport Mexicos, which produced a wonderful battle between the actor Jeremy Lloyd and Noel Edmonds. The latter clipped the former into a spin on the last lap right in front of us. Cracking stuff.

A total of thirty-four cars were entered for the Grand Prix, chasing twenty-five spaces on the grid. In those days, apart from the core teams and drivers, private entries came and went, and sometimes the main teams would run an extra driver if they felt like it. One hopeful was the Italian female driver, Lella Lombardi, who attempted to become the first woman to qualify for a World Championship Grand Prix. She impressed with her handling of the privately run Brabham-Ford BT42, but a broken gearbox thwarted her efforts in the final session.

The Russians are coming. A novel addition to the runners in the 1974 Triplex Production Saloon Car Championship was the inclusion of two Russian Moskvich 412s for Peter Jopp and Tony Stubbs. The pair finished third and second respectively in their class, behind the Sunbeam Imp of Simon Watson. There were only four entries in the class, mind …

Barry Foley, in his St. Bruno Holbay Roughcutter, gets it all wrong exiting Bottom Bend in the ShellSport Clubmans race.

The F5000 cars were always a glorious sight at Brands, as demonstrated here by the Lola T330 of Ian Ashley leading the Chevron B28 of Teddy Pilette and Bob Evans' Lola T332 out of Druids. Evans went on to win the race from Brian Redman, with Ashley in third. Pilette was seventh.

The VDS Chevron-Chevrolet B28 of fourth-placed finisher Peter Gethin sits in the paddock after the race.

FordSport Day again! Colin Hawker in the DFV-powered Toleman Capri finished second in the *Daily Mail* Challenge Race for Ford-engined special and production saloon cars.

Opposite page, clockwise from top: Heat winner Syd Fox (Hawke DL11) was one of the masters of Formula Ford in the seventies and is seen here leading Rob Wicken (Merlyn Mk17A) into Druids; Danny Burritt spins his Titan Mk 6 at Druids during the first Formula Ford heat; an angry pack of Formula Ford cars muscles its way through Druids in the first of the BOC Golden Helmet heats. Tim Brise (26) took the distinctive Elden Scholar Mk 10X to fifth place.

The ShellSport Escort Mexicos always provided good entertainment, and the programme featured a ladies event - with the winner receiving an in-car cassette player! This is the Italian F5000 driver Lella Lombardi leading the field at Druids.

Tiff Needell in his Elden Scholar Mk 10C finished third in his heat.

Motor Racing at Brands Hatch in the seventies

Fast and furious. The three leading cars exit Druids in one of the four Formula Ford races that day.

To mark the occasion, Ford brought along one of its 3.4 litre works Capri RS3100s, prepared by Ford of Cologne and driven by Dieter Glemser, from the European Saloon Car Championship for a demonstration run.

Unfortunately, it disgraced itself, the engine erupting in a cloud of smoke …

… and the car coasting to a halt at Druids. There were plenty of marshals and photographers on hand to offer advice as to the problem!

The *Evening News* Showbiz Challenge, with celebrities in identical Escort Mexicos, provided plenty of entertainment during the lunch break on Grand Prix day. This is the actor Jeremy Lloyd spinning on the last lap after a race-long duel with disc jockey Noel Edmonds, who took the win.

The Formula Atlantic brigade was the first support race for the Grand Prix meeting that year. Peter Wardle in his STP Surtees TS15 is in the middle of the frame, and just behind him is the Wella-sponsored March 74B of American Ted Wentz.

Niki Lauda, in the Ferrari 312B3, led initially, followed by Jody Scheckter's Tyrrell-Ford 007, and the other Ferrari of Clay Regazzoni. A few laps from the end Lauda's right rear tyre began to slowly deflate. He kept going as long as he could until Scheckter swept by into the lead with just five laps left to run. Lauda pitted for a new tyre one lap from the end but, as he tried to re-join, the pit lane was blocked with a course car and a crowd of people. He was classified ninth but later awarded fifth place on appeal.

Long distance sports car racing returned after a year's absence at the end of September and, on a bright autumn day, the all-conquering Matra MS670Cs dominated the event. It was a good day if your name was Jean-Pierre, since J-P Jarier and J-P Beltoise drove the winning car, beating their team mates by just 2.8 seconds.

The final round of the Rothmans European F5000 Championship took place in October, with victory in the race going to Vern Schuppan in the Chevron-Chevrolet B24/8. The event marked the end of Rothmans' involvement in motor racing, which was the first tobacco company in Britain to support the sport, back in 1961.

Grand Prix time and Niki Lauda (Ferrari) leads eventual winner Jody Scheckter (Tyrrell),
Ronnie Peterson (JPS Lotus), Clay Regazzoni (Ferrari), and Carlos Reuteman (Brabham) on
the first lap.

Patrick Depailler (Tyrrell) and Arturo Merzario (Iso Marlboro) lead the midfield runners
around Druids.

Niki Lauda dominated the 1974 John Player British Grand Prix until six laps from the end when he picked up a puncture, losing the lead to Jody Scheckter's Tyrrell. Lauda pitted one lap from the end to change the tyre, but was unable to re-join the race because an official car was blocking the end of the pit lane and he was classified ninth. He was later awarded fifth place, which is where he would have finished had he been able to re-join.

Ronnie Peterson in a JPS Lotus-Ford 72E was always an evocative sight, but by 1974 the car was into its fifth season of racing and had lost its edge over the competition. Despite winning in Monaco earlier in the year, Peterson was out of luck at Brands Hatch, finishing tenth after suffering a puncture.

One of the more unusual runners that day was the Trojan-Ford T103 of Tim Schenken. The Australian qualified at the back of the grid and retired on lap seven.

The French driver François Migault was an extra BRM runner, partnering Jean-Pierre Beltoise and Henri Pescarolo. The rear wing of his P160E fell off partway through the race but he persevered and finished sixteenth and last, twelve laps behind the winner.

It was easy to gain access to the Formula One paddock in those days, where Ronnie Peterson's JPS Lotus-Ford 72E sits, minus its nose cone …

… as does the Texaco-Marlboro McLaren-Ford M23 of Denny Hulme. The cars have had their slick race tyres removed and treaded tyres fitted for transportation.

No, your eyes are not deceiving you, it is a caravan race. This is Andrew Higton in a Vauxhall VX 4/90 pulling a Bailey prototype. Higton won the event at the EMI Records/Radio Luxembourg day meeting and, yes, they did fall over if they went round the corners too fast.

This is the traditional August Bank Holiday meeting, and for some bizarre reason a race between British and Dutch drivers, in ShellSport Escort Mexicos, is on the bill. Fred Frankenhout (9) is being unceremoniously elbowed out of the way by Damian Magee (14).

The ShellSport Mexicos were once again tasked with providing the entertainment for the masses at the EMI Records/Radio Luxembourg day, with a selection of pop stars and disc jockeys at the wheel. This is Radio Luxembourg DJ Tony Prince experiencing a tad too much oversteer at Druids. He did this every lap.

The feature race on Bank Holiday Monday was, as usual, a round of the Rothmans F5000 European Championship. The ShellSport-Luxembourg sponsored Lola-Chevrolet T330 of Ian Ashley finished fourth on this occasion.

On lap five of the F5000 encounter, the South African driver Eddie Keizan was clipped by eventual winner Tony Dean, damaging the nose of the Embassy Racing Lola-Chevrolet T332.

Matra dominated the sports car Championship in 1974 and the Brands Hatch round was no exception. This is race winner Jean-Pierre Jarier, in the MS670C which he shared with Jean-Pierre Beltoise.

The nearest challengers to the all-conquering Matras were the pair of Gulf-Ford GR7s. The number three car, driven by Derek Bell (shown here) and David Hobbs, finished in third place, albeit eleven laps in arrears. The sister GR7 of Vern Schuppan and Reine Wisell retired with a broken driveshaft.

The abandoned Chevron Ford B23 of Richard Robarts and Hector Rebaque at Westfield Bend.

After being dropped from the calendar in 1973, long-distance sports car racing returned to the track in 1974, albeit later in the year than the traditional April events. September saw the British Airways 1000 which attracted a healthy entry. The Martini-backed Group 5 Porsche Carrera Turbo of Herbert Muller and Gijs van Lennep, which finished fifth, is seen leading the Chevron B26 of John Hine and Ian Grob, who came in ninth.

The glorious Herbert Muller/Gijs van Lennep Martini Porsche again. The car qualified tenth and finished fifth.

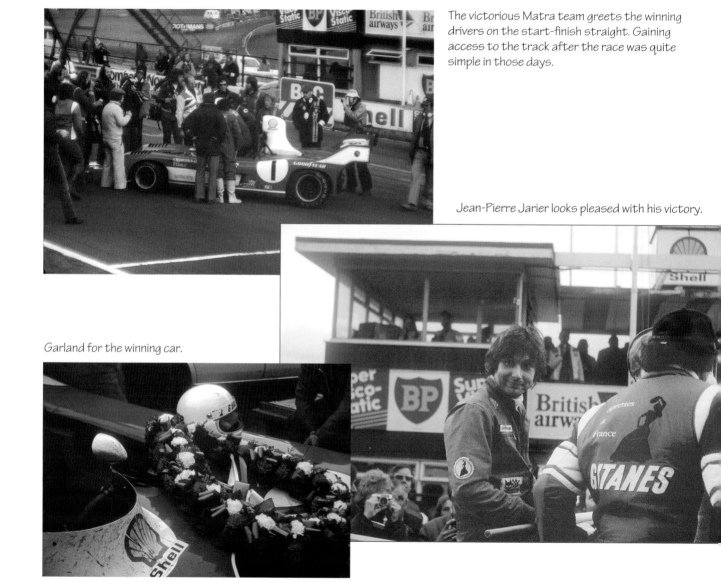

The victorious Matra team greets the winning drivers on the start-finish straight. Gaining access to the track after the race was quite simple in those days.

Jean-Pierre Jarier looks pleased with his victory.

Garland for the winning car.

The Motor Show 200, held in October, was traditionally the last major meeting of the year.

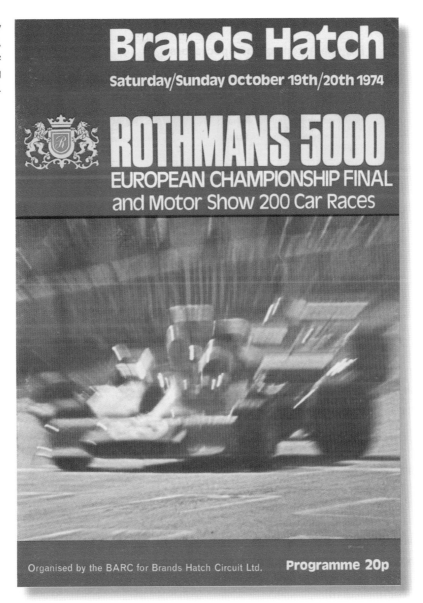

Brands Hatch

Saturday/Sunday October 19th/20th 1974

ROTHMANS 5000
EUROPEAN CHAMPIONSHIP FINAL
and Motor Show 200 Car Races

Organised by the BARC for Brands Hatch Circuit Ltd.   **Programme 20p**

1975

1975 was the track's 25th anniversary, and, to celebrate, both the Club and Grand Prix circuits were completely re-surfaced during January and February; the first time the whole track had been covered in one go since it opened.

The season kicked off in March with a BBC Radio One Championship car meeting which gave a mouth-watering taster for the year ahead. Tony Brise won the main race of the day, the Formula Atlantic encounter, while the Formula Fords provided the usual spectacle.

It was cold at the Race of Champions in March, but the race provided a popular win for Welshman Tom Pryce in the Shadow-Ford DN5/2A. A flurry of snow just before the start caused us to turn our collars up, and the drivers to switch from dry to wet tyres, and then back again. At the start Jacky Ickx in the JPS Lotus-Ford 72 took the lead, but by the end of the lap it was Jody Scheckter in the Tyrrell-Ford 007 out in front. It stayed

The BBC, in the form of Radio One, sponsored the whole Production Saloon Car Championship that year, again demonstrating the links between the pop world and motor racing. This is Colin Folwell in the Corbeau GT Seats Vauxhall Magnum at Druids.

March 1975 saw the season opener in the form of the BBC Radio One Championship Car race meeting, which included a Special Saloon Car race. This allowed any modification, provided the shape of the cars remained original. Davina Galica, the former ladies British skiing champion, made her race debut, and is seen here powering her Escort through Paddock Bend during practice. In the race she went off the track here.

this way for some time, but Pryce moved up to second and began to eat away at the Tyrrell's lead. Just as he looked like getting into a position to pass, the engine on the Tyrrell tightened and Scheckter headed for the pits. Pryce reeled off the remaining thirteen laps to score his first, and only, F1 victory.

Easter was a busy time if you were a F5000 runner; on Good Friday you were at Oulton Park, having practised on the Thursday for the second round of the European F5000 Championship, and then it was a quick run south to Brands to practise on Easter Sunday for the Bank Holiday Monday meeting. The trusted Chevrolet 5 litre engine had been the mainstay of F5000 for many years, but Ford had introduced a V6 which David Purley used in the back of his Lec Chevron B30 to good effect.

The track celebrated its 25th birthday in April with a typical, well organised, eight-race meeting for Formula

The great exponent of Special Saloons in those days was the legendary Gerry Marshall. He dominated this race, as usual, in his Dealer Team Vauxhall Firenza.

Tony Brise in the Modus Ford M1 leads the Southern Organs Formula Atlantic race on a streaming wet track. It is sad to think that by the end of the year Brise would have graduated to Formula One with Graham Hill's team, only to be killed in a plane crash, along with Hill and other team members, in November.

Different shape, same antics. The fleet of ShellSport Escorts had been replaced by a brand new set boasting the Mk II bodyshell. Here, Terry Jackson leads John Layland, David Wooton and Phil Clarke.

Atlantics (won by Tony Brise), Group One touring cars, special saloons, FF2000 and, in memory of the circuit's early days, Formula Junior cars. There was even a ShellSport Escort race for 'golden oldie' drivers, won by Paddy Hopkirk. The sun shone but attendance was poor.

The August Bank Holiday meeting had to be switched from the GP circuit to the club circuit after the track surface started breaking up during practice. Even so, the crowd was treated to a real spectacle as Alan Jones in the Thursdays/RAM March-Ford 751 fought a ding-dong battle with Tony Brise's Theodore Lola-Chevrolet T332. Brise had taken pole, and led most of the race, but was slowed with a puncture. Jones edged ever closer and, with three laps to go, made a dive down the inside at Paddock to take the lead. He then broke the circuit lap record. Brise pressed on and the pair had lapped the rest of the field by the end.

In October, MCD announced that, in 1976, the F5000 championship would be replaced by a new series open to all single-seaters up to five litres in capacity, thereby

Sports car fans had a treat in June in the form of a round of the European 2 litre Sports Car Championship. The event was sponsored by Encyclopaedia Britannica and dubbed the Britannica 2000. This is the immaculate March-Hart 75S of John Lepp with Martin Raymond's Fisons-backed Chevron-Hart B31 in the background.

The beautiful Warsteiner-backed Toj-BMW SG03 of German driver Paul Keller.

It looks just like a Ferrari but it's not. This is the Scuderia Nordvest Osella PA3 with 'Gianfranco' at the wheel. The car finished a respectable fifth.

Guy Edwards steers his CI Caravans Lola-Hart T390 through Bottom Bend on his way to second place in the Britannica 2000.

Motor Racing at Brands Hatch in the seventies

including F1 and F2 cars. As a result, the annual Motor Show 200 saw Brands kiss goodbye to F5000 after six seasons. The event neatly book ended the series as Peter Gethin, who had won the first British F5000 race, also took victory in the last, driving the Lola-Chevrolet T400.

Later that year the motor racing world was shocked when Graham Hill and his young protégé, Tony Brise, who had enjoyed so much success at Brands Hatch, and other members of the Embassy-Hill Formula One team, were killed in a plane crash near Elstree aerodrome on 29 November.

Opposite: (Top) Mike Smith, who later went on enjoy success as a disc jockey and television presenter, not only raced but was employed as press officer at Brands for a while. This is him taking a tight line on the exit of Druids in his 3 litre Ford Capri MkII in the production saloon event on his way to a class win. A line of cement dust on the track is evidence of oil spilled in a previous race. (Bottom) The main event and Teddy Pilette leads the Formula 5000 field in his Team VDS Lola Chevrolet T400. Pilette enjoyed a spirited dice for the lead with Tony Brise before he retired with suspension failure.

A sunny August Bank Holiday Monday, and Caldwell Smythe is on his way to winning the Clubmans Sports Car race in his Mallock U2 Ford Swindon Mk. 16. The U2s were so named because you too could have one ...

Star of the day was future F1 World Champion Alan Jones, who won in his Thursdays/RAM March-Ford 751 after a mesmeric drive during which he caught and passed the Lola of race leader Tony Brise, breaking the outright circuit lap record on his way.

Stuffed it! One sponsor which raised eyebrows was Durex, the contraceptive manufacturer. Jokes abounded about hoping the car didn't get any punctures, but this was a serious effort and the company enjoyed its high profile. Here, Richard Scott retires the team's Lola-Chevrolet T400.

Tony Brise in the Theodore Racing Lola-Chevrolet T332. The Embassy F1 driver finished second to Alan Jones, the two drivers lapping everyone else in the race.

In the 1600-2500cc class of the British Touring Car Championship, it was the Triumph Dolomite Sprints of Andy Rouse (40) and Roger Bell (41) that provided the entertainment in the late afternoon sunshine. Rouse won the class whilst Bell finished third.

1976

Major changes were made to the circuit in 1976. The entry to Paddock Bend was made tighter (the old track remained in place as a run-off area), and the whole of Bottom Straight was moved into South Bank. This allowed a flat, tarmacked area, which would serve as a paddock for F1 cars, to be created immediately behind the pits, meaning that the F1 teams would be completely self-contained during the Grand Prix.

On the long circuit the old bridge which spanned the track at the exit of Kidney Corner was removed, and additional Armco barriers and increased run-off areas were provided at all corners. Despite all the alterations, the length of the circuit changed by just sixty-four yards (fifty-eight metres).

It was the pit area where the changes were most noticeable, however. The complex was completely modernised with a new control tower overlooking a pit road that had been doubled in length. In addition, thirty-seven new garages, with running water and electricity in each, had been erected together with a new changing-room block.

The show jumper Ann Moore tried her hand at Formula Ford 2000. Her debut was inauspicious as this incident, where she has managed to spin her Elden Mk 18 on the approach to Druids and parked it broadside across the track.

But she wasn't the only one to get it wrong that day. Giancarlo Martini locked-up his rear brakes and crashed his Scuderia Everest Ferrari 312T at exactly the same spot on the warm-up lap to the 1976 Race of Champions.

The approach to Druids was turning into a dead-car parking lot. Carlos Pace, standing on the bank opposite, has just retired his Martini Brabham-Alfa Romeo BT45 with fuel injection problems after only seven laps.

The end of the race, and Martini's Ferrari 312T is removed by the marshals.

Jacky Ickx drove the Williams-Ford FW05 (an ex-Hesketh 308C) to third, despite the visor on his helmet splitting in half partway through the race.

The radical six-wheeled Tyrrell-Ford P34. A mid-week tyre testing session, organised by Goodyear and held at the circuit in June, was the first chance the British public had to view the extraordinary new machine.

Motor Racing at Brands Hatch in the seventies

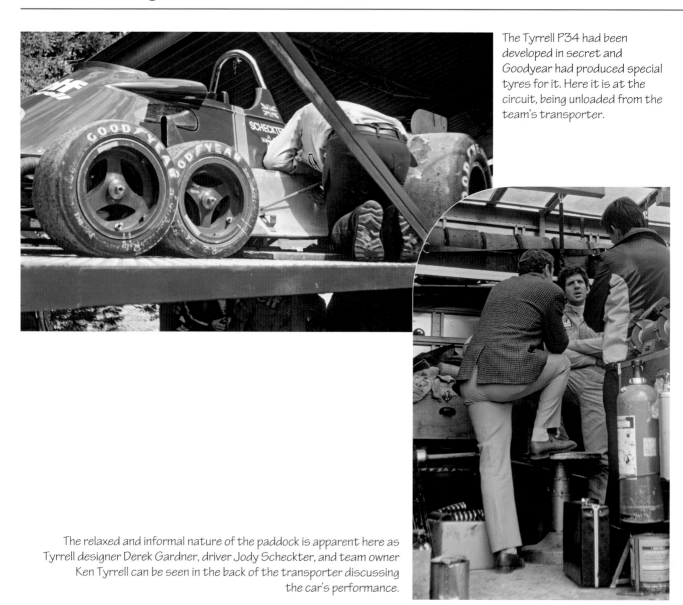

The Tyrrell P34 had been developed in secret and Goodyear had produced special tyres for it. Here it is at the circuit, being unloaded from the team's transporter.

The relaxed and informal nature of the paddock is apparent here as Tyrrell designer Derek Gardner, driver Jody Scheckter, and team owner Ken Tyrrell can be seen in the back of the transporter discussing the car's performance.

June, and the ShellSport European Formula 5000 brigade are out in force again. This is David Purley in the LEC Refrigeration Chevron B30 with a 3.4 litre Ford V6 engine. Purley extended his lead in the Championship by winning the race after a thrilling wheel-to-wheel dice with Damien Magee's March-Ford 751.

Rule changes meant that F1, F2 and F Atlantic cars were now eligible for the ShellSport 5000 Championship. Mike Wilds took this Formula One Shadow-Ford DN3B/2A to fourth place.

The old paddock was also improved, being moved off the slope behind Paddock Bend to the flat area at the bottom of the hill. For the spectators more concrete terracing was installed, a new shop complex planned and, to the relief of many of us, the catering contract changed.

The work provided the opportunity to rename some of the corners; Bottom Bend became Graham Hill Bend, Bottom Straight became Cooper Straight, Kidney Corner was now Surtees, and the right-hander immediately after it on the Club circuit became McLaren. The last part of Clearways was renamed Clark Curve, and Top Straight was now Brabham Straight. Out on the long circuit, Portobello Straight became the Derek Minter Straight.

The work on the circuit was completed in time for the Race of Champions in March which produced a popular win for James Hunt in the Marlboro McLaren-Ford M23. The race had been due to be televised by the BBC but the corporation withdrew its cameras the day before on the grounds that the level of advertising on the cars was unacceptable.

In May spectators were able to attend a mid-week Formula One test, organised by tyre company Goodyear. Entry was free, and the atmosphere easy and relaxed, with the F1 teams based in the old paddock, allowing the public access.

The test session was just a warm-up, of course, for the true highlight of the year, the John Player British Grand Prix in July. Admission was £5 (£4 in advance), with children £1. Apart from the racing, which included BP Formula Three and Keith Prowse British Touring Car Championship events, we were treated to displays by the Pitts Special aerobatic plane, the Red Devils parachute team, the Blue Eagles Army helicopter team, and various on-track demonstrations. You got your money's worth in those days.

The Special Saloon event in June was won this time by the Mini Countryman driven by Ginger Marshall in the 851-1000cc class.

Alo Lawler has just lost the wheel on his Formula Atlantic Chevron-Ford B29. The errant wheel parted company from the car as he rounded Druids, and bounced toward the barrier on the outside of the circuit. Thankfully it did not end up in the crowd.

Some things never change, and the sight of a Mini cocking a wheel was just as common in 1976 as it ever was. This is Pete Knipe, who finished third in the up-to 850cc class in his BMC Mini in the Special Saloon race.

Motor Racing at Brands Hatch in the seventies

The McLaren mechanics are working on James Hunt's M23 in its pit garage at the British Grand Prix.

This was the year that 77,000 fans made their feelings known in no uncertain terms after the two Ferraris of Niki Lauda and Clay Regazzoni clashed at Paddock Bend on the opening lap, resulting in local hero James Hunt being punted high into the air, and the race being stopped.

I was sitting in the startline grandstand when it was announced that Hunt would not be allowed to restart. A loud jeer went up and I remember seeing the people on the grid, Hunt included, turn to see what the commotion from the grandstands was all about. Then the boos began, followed by the stomping of feet and the slow, deliberate clapping of hands. It dawned on the officials that if they didn't allow Hunt to start they would have a riot on their hands. The decision was reversed - they could worry about the legality of it later. Hunt raced, passed his arch-rival Niki Lauda's Ferrari 312T2, and won the race. We went home happy although Hunt was later disqualified.

The Formula Ford Festival, which had been a popular event at Snetterton for the previous three years, was moved to Brands Hatch for 1976. The meeting was then expanded, with the addition of an extra round of the ShellSport 5000 Championship, to turn it into a Tribute to James Hunt meeting, in recognition of him winning the World Drivers' Championship. David Purley dominated an exciting, but very wet, race from the Penske PC3 of Derek Bell, while Derek Daly in a Hawke DL17 was the outright Formula Ford winner.

At the end of qualifying for the British Grand Prix the pits were just as accessible as the paddock, and members of the public could watch the mechanics working on the cars. This is one of the Brabham-Alfa Romeo BT45s in its garage.

Motor Racing at Brands Hatch in the seventies

James Hunt in his Marlboro McLaren-Ford M23 is lined-up on pole position just before the start of the 1976 British Grand Prix.

The flag has gone down and Niki Lauda in the Ferrari 312T2 has got the jump on Hunt as they power away towards Paddock Bend.

It was to be a bitter-sweet affair for James Hunt. He was initially knocked off at the first corner, managed to make the restart and went on to win the race, only to be excluded from the results later on.

After a collision at Paddock Bend on the first lap, the Grand Prix was stopped and the cars returned to the grid. Alan Jones' Durex Surtees-Ford TS19 and the McLaren-Ford M23 of James Hunt's team mate Jochen Mass are being pushed into position.

The end of the race and Hunt has won - for the moment at least. He celebrates his victory in the usual style, spraying the crowd below with champagne.

Race day and the grid for the Keith Prowse British Saloon Car Championship race is about to get away. On the front row are the Ford Capris of Tom Walkinshaw, Gordon Spice, and Chris Craft. Eventual winner Vince Woodman, in another Capri, is back on row three.

Brands Hatch hosted rounds of many different championships, including Formula Three, during the year.

Brands Hatch

Sunday, 23rd May, 1976

BP Formula 3 Championship Meeting

Organised by the BARC for Brands Hatch Circuit Limited

Programme 25p

Formula Ford races were the staple diet of many meetings at the circuit. The August Bank Holiday event in 1976 boasted no fewer than four - three on the Sunday and another on the Monday. Here, Chris Dobson gets off the line cleanly in his Merlyn Scholar Mk 20A.

1977

In 1977 the British Racing and Sports Car Club (BRSCC) relocated from its Chiswick HQ to offices at Brands, causing much controversy among the members. The strong links with the circuit, achieved by being on-site, mirrored those enjoyed by the British Automobile Racing Club (BARC) at Thruxton and the British Racing Drivers' Club (BRDC) at Silverstone.

Development of the new paddock area was completed, and over 1000 trees were planted between the areas of hard standing. The intention was for these to be used as garden areas, but the niceties of this idea were lost on competitors who parked on them and emptied their waste oil onto the ground.

The entry for the Race of Champions this year was poor compared to others, but the weather was good and a large crowd turned out to see the action.

The Race of Champions, and the Brabham mechanics are working to get the sole BT45 of John Watson, who qualified on pole position, ready for the race. A pit lane walkabout, for holders of paddock passes, was common at events like this.

The Tyrrell mechanics are working on Ronnie Peterson's six-wheeled P34 in its pit garage. The two-and-a-quarter hour pits walkabout on the morning of the race gave spectators plenty of time to observe the preparation of the cars.

John Watson (Brabham-Alfa BT45) was on pole ahead of Mario Andretti (JPS Lotus-Ford 78), and James Hunt (Marlboro McLaren-Ford M23). At the start Andretti and Hunt shot ahead and fought it out all race, until the Lotus driver retired seven laps from the end, leaving the victory to Hunt.

By this time I wasn't just spectating at Brands and other tracks - I had friends who had also caught the motor racing bug, and had decided to compete. The beauty of having friends who raced was that not only could you get free tickets to the events, but you enjoyed access to the pits as well.

Enjoying an outing in his Formula Ford Merlyn Mk 11/25A in May was my friend Alan, who was having a more successful time than when he'd made his racing debut at the track earlier in the year. On that occasion he'd lined up on the back of the grid, the flag dropped,

One of the support events for the Race of Champions in 1977 was for Formula Ford 2000 cars. Here, the field streams out of Druids Bend and down towards Graham Hill Bend, formerly Bottom Bend.

Mario Andretti in the JPS Lotus-Ford 78 leads James Hunt's McLaren-Ford M23, John Watson's Brabham-Alfa BT45, the Wolf-Ford WR1 of Jody Scheckter, and the Tyrrell-Ford P34 of Ronnie Peterson. Andretti led until seven laps from home when a faulty ignition switch caused him to retire, leaving Hunt to take the victory.

and the field roared off towards Paddock. Except for Alan – Alan roared off towards Clearways. In the heat of the moment, and having previously competed in Autocross events driving a Mini, he selected gear as the flag went up. The trouble was that the position of first gear in a Mini corresponded to reverse in the Merlyn, with the resulting embarrassment. Oh, how we laughed …

The August Bank Holiday weekend was an unhappy one at the track; the Australian driver Brian McQuire and a fire marshal, John Thorpe, were killed during practice for the ShellSport 5000 race. McQuire's car crashed at Stirling's Bend on the long circuit, flipped, and landed where three marshals were standing. The race was won by Emilio de Villota in a McLaren-Ford M23, while Davina Galica, who had made her racing debut at the circuit in 1974, finished a fine third, after leading at one stage, in her Surtees-Ford TS19.

Cars for one of the Formula Three heats line up behind the pits in May 1977. Ian Ashley is in a Lola T570 on the left, Ian Flux is in the middle in his Ralt RT1, and on the right is the Chevron B38 of Patrick Gaillard.

Geoff Brabham, son of three-times World Champion Jack, lines up in his Ralt-Toyota RT1 on the outside of the three-two-three grid for the first Formula Three qualifying race of the day ...

... alongside him is Eje Elgh in a Chevron-Toyota B38 who went on to win the heat ...

... while on pole position is the March-Triumph 733 of Ian Taylor. Three makes of car occupying the three front row slots on the grid.

The World Championship of Makes sports cars returned to the circuit in September for a six-hour race, but the entry was poor, the series having struggled throughout the year. Even so, with Jacky Ickx and Jochen Mass in a Martini Porsche 935-77, and Ronnie Peterson and Hans Stuck in a BMW 320 Turbo, it looked like being a good race. The weather was atrocious though, and Stuck fell off the road after only five laps, having just taken the lead from Ickx. After an hour-and-a-quarter the race was stopped, conditions having deteriorated to the point where cars were spinning off everywhere. Us poor spectators were already soaked through and glad of the opportunity to find shelter and to try and warm up. After an hour the race was restarted, the rain having stopped, and Ickx and Mass won from the Manfred Schurti and Edgar Doren Porsche.

In November, the Brazilian Chico Serra won the Formula Ford Festival, dominating the event in his Van Diemen as Derek Daly had the year before.

The Modified Sports Car contenders line up in the afternoon sunshine behind the pits, headed by the Davrian Mk 7s of Pat Longhurst and Bob Jarvis.

Motor Racing at Brands Hatch in the seventies

Another day, another Formula Ford race. Alan Hall gets his Merlyn Mk 11/25A off the line. The cross on the rear of the car marks him out as a novice to his fellow drivers.

A Formula Three competitor leaves the pit lane as the rest of the field swarms towards Paddock Bend.

Accidents will happen. The Austin Healey Sprite of Garry Wilson has crashed on Cooper Straight, just behind the pits, during the Modified Sports Car encounter.

World Championship Sports Car racing returned to the Kent circuit in September 1977 in the shape of a six-hour endurance event. The weather wasn't kind, however, and caught out many of the competitors, including the driver of this De Tomaso Pantera who has spun exiting Druids.

The Ronnie Peterson and Hans Stuck BMW 320 Turbo looked as if it would provide Porsche with strong opposition but, unfortunately, Stuck went off the road only five laps into the race, just after he had taken the lead. Notice the water streaming off the car as it heads down the hill out of Druids.

Stars of the race were Jacky Ickx and Jochen Mass in this beautiful Martini-backed Porsche 935/77. The pair took pole position and led almost the entire race.

Opposite: (Inset) The circuit held a meeting to celebrate the Queen's Silver Jubilee in June 1977, with sponsorship from Capital Radio.
(Main) Out in the country, a Porsche 935 produces a spectacular 'flame-out' as it drops through Dingle Dell.

Shell *SPORT*
International

In association with the EVENING NEWS

Brands Hatch

MONDAY, 29th AUGUST, 1977

Programme 30p

Organised by the BRSCC

The ShellSport 5000 series, open to all single-seater cars up to five litres in capacty, was the successor to Formula 5000. The following year it, too, would be replaced.

1978

An even-numbered year meant that the Grand Prix was at Brands again, and the circuit swung into action with a raft of improvements for the big event. Around the long circuit double Armco barrier replaced all the old sleepers, and wider run-off areas and spectator banks were built. Double Armco was also installed from Paddock to Druids, and Druids to Cooper Straight, and a new spectator slope was put in at McLaren Bend. From the spectator's point of view the news that most of the toilets would be connected to a new drainage system was probably the most welcome.

In national racing the ShellSport 5000 series gave way to the Aurora-AFX Formula One Championship (although F2 cars were also eligible), the second round of which was held at Brands on Easter Monday. Tony Trimmer, in a McLaren-Ford M23, was the victor, having already triumphed at Oulton Park on Good Friday.

The first week of June saw F1 cars testing mid-week on the GP circuit, in preparation for the forthcoming Grand Prix in July. Interest centred around the new Brabham-Alfa BT46B fan car, driven by Niki Lauda. The car had only broken cover the week before, and featured a large fan at the rear. Claimed to be there to cool the engine, it actually sucked the car down onto the track, thereby improving grip. Lauda managed only a few laps before the car broke down, its rear being quickly covered by mechanics so that no one could photograph it.

As was usual, a group of friends and I assembled at the circuit the day before the John Player Grand Prix in July to watch practice, and in the afternoon we waited to see the Formula Three encounter, which included a young Nelson Piquet.

If you are a photographer, you always hope to get the perfect shot or capture an incident as it happens. At the start, watching from the top of Paddock Bend, we saw

The European Saloon Car Championship visited the circuit in March 1978 for a 120 lap race. Tom Walkinshaw and the Italian driver Umberto Grano took the victory in this 3.2-litre BMW CSL.

Easter Monday and the Production Saloons are on the bill, demonstrating a number of ways to negotiate the Druids hairpin. These are Tony Lanfranchi (Opel Commodore) Gerry Marshall (Dolomite Sprint), and Alan Minshaw (Opel Commodore).

James Hunt in the McLaren-Ford M26 powers through Stirling's Bend on the long circuit during F1 tyre testing.

Formula 5000 was replaced this year by the Aurora AFX Formula One Championship for F1 and F2 cars. Here Guy Edwards spins his March 761 as the McLaren M23 of Tony Trimmer passes. The pair had been dicing for the lead - never more than a second apart - with Edwards in front, but they tangled at Druids, Edwards dropping to fourth and Trimmer going on to win.

the Nova of Satoru Nakajima barrel-roll through the air before crashing back to the ground. Nelson Piquet and Chico Serra had touched, sending Piquet across the path of the pack with the inevitable pile-up. Incredibly, no one was injured but it was one of the most violent accidents I had ever witnessed. Unfortunately, I'd left my camera back in the car for that race ...

The Grand Prix threw up a surprise, with victory going to Carlos Reutemann in the Ferrari 312T3. Apart from the racing, the crowd was also entertained by the Red Arrows, performing their famous cross-over right over the centre of the natural bowl of the circuit, and the

event marked the first use of the new Kentagon - a six-sided entertainment building at the top of the hill above the old paddock. Although the building was far from finished, the bar was specially opened for the Grand Prix weekend.

One of the boldest initiatives of John Webb and Motor Circuit Developments was to bring the United States Auto Club's Indy cars to Britain to race on consecutive weekends at Silverstone and Brands Hatch. Alas, the experiment was not a success. Both races attracted only half the expected number of spectators, and the Brands event, switched at the last minute to

Another F1 mid-week tyre testing session took place this year, a month before the Grand Prix and Gilles Villeneuve is seen at Paddock Hill Bend in his Ferrari 312T3.

Another driver taking advantage of the pre-race test was Jody Scheckter in the Wolf-Ford WR5.

the Club circuit, turned into a boring procession. Danny Ongais (Danny On-the-gas as the commentator dubbed him) was leading by over a lap when his Parnelli retired close to the finish. Rick Mears and Tom Sneva, therefore, made it a Penske 1-2. Despite the lack of close racing, it was a glorious autumn day, the cars made a fabulous sight, and it was good to see some different machinery and drivers for a change. A brave idea, just a pity more people didn't come to see it.

The tyre tests provided the only appearance in the UK of the Brabham-Alfa Romeo BT46B fan car, with Niki Lauda at the wheel. The Gordon Murray-designed machine featured a large fan at the rear, officially to help cool the engine, but in reality to suck the car onto the ground, thereby massively improving grip. The car won the Swedish Grand Prix but was outlawed before the next race took place.

1978 was the year that Mario Andretti and Ronnie Peterson in their JPS Lotus-Ford 79s swept all before them, except at Brands Hatch that is, where both cars retired. This is Andretti during qualifying for the Grand Prix. Note the lack of tobacco sponsorship which was removed for the British and German races.

Overseas visitors. The United States Automobile Club (USAC) Indy cars visited these shores in 1978 with back-to-back races at Silverstone and Brands Hatch. At the last minute it was decided to switch the Brands race to the short circuit, which resulted in it being renamed the Indy circuit to commemorate the event. Here, Bobby Unser in an Eagle and A. J. Foyt in a Coyote round Paddock.

The Indy cars provided a magnificent sight as they set off for the 100 lap race with Rick Mears in his Penske leading Gordon Johncock (Wildcat), Danny Ongais (Parnelli), and the rest of the field. Unfortunately, attendance was poor and the race itself turned into a procession.

1979

The international season at Brands, in the last year of the decade, should have kicked off on 18 March with the Race of Champions, but the event was postponed at the last minute due to the expected imminent arrival of snow. The decision was taken the Thursday before the scheduled date, and the snow duly arrived the following day. However, it was too late to stop the Ferrari team which had already turned up. The race was re-scheduled for April 15 - Easter Sunday - and the round of the Aurora AFX Formula One Championship that was due to take place that day was incorporated into the main event. The entry for the main race had been badly affected by the date change, and the twelve Aurora runners were a welcome addition to the otherwise sparse field of just seven Grand Prix cars.

The main point of interest was Mario Andretti's brand new, and radical, Lotus-Ford 80, the car designed to run without any wings. Testing proved that the theory didn't work, however, and the car appeared at Brands sprouting a rear aerofoil but still devoid of nose wings. Problems with the new car meant that Andretti had to use his trusty old 79 to qualify, and duly put it on pole. He tried the 80 again on race morning but elected to run the older car. Fellow front row man Niki Lauda, in the Brabham-Alfa BT48, led initially before stopping for new tyres after only eight laps. Andretti took over at the front but was passed by Gilles Villeneuve, in the old Ferrari 312T3, who went on to win.

The sparse entry meant the name Race of Champions was a bit of a misnomer. Still, it was an enjoyable meeting, and a busy weekend for me as I headed off to Thruxton the next day for the traditional Easter Monday Formula Two bash.

Standing at a track like Thruxton, an old airfield

John Player terminated its sponsorship of the Lotus team at the end of 1978, and so for the '79 season the cars were decked out in Martini livery. Mario Andretti practised this brand new and radical Lotus-Ford 80 at the Race of Champions, but elected to race the previous year's 79 model, finishing third.

Niki Lauda started the Parmalat Brabham-Alfa Romeo BT48 from the front row, and held the lead before having to stop for new tyres after only eight laps. He finished fifth.

circuit like Silverstone, reinforced what made Brands such a wonderful spectator circuit. Thruxton is fast but flat, and you only see the cars for a brief period as they fly past. Even at the complex or the chicane, both spectacular viewing points, visibility is limited compared to the natural bowl of Brands Hatch.

The only other major international event that year was the six-hour sports car race in August. The event was a Porsche walkover, with victory going to the four-year-old 908/4 model of Reinhold Jost and Volkert Merl. The Kremer team was a last minute entry with two of its Le Mans-winning Porsche 935 K3s; Klaus Ludwig and Axel Plankenhorn put up a spirited fight to take second, but couldn't match the older 908/4.

In August, the Aurora AFX Formula One Championship returned to the Kent circuit for the

Gilles Villeneuve won the 1979 Race of Champions in his Ferrari 312T3. The entry was poor with only seven World Championship runners taking part. The field was made up with entrants from the domestic Aurora AFX Formula One Championship.

A feature of the 1979 season was the BMW County Championship for identical BMW 323i saloons with drivers representing different English counties. Win Percy (Avon) leads Barrie Williams (Gloucestershire), Tony Dron (Nottinghamshire), and the rest of the field round Paddock on the first lap of the supporting race for the August Six Hour sports car event. The trio finished in the same order.

traditional Bank Holiday meeting. The Argentine driver Ricardo Zunino in an Arrows-Ford A1B established himself at the start with a lead he would never lose. Behind him Guy Edwards in a Fittipaldi-Ford F5A battled throughout the race, with David Kennedy's Wolf-Ford WR6, just holding him off to the flag.

As ever, the seventh Formula Ford Festival, and the fourth to be held at Brands, was an elimination event with eight seven-lap heats on Saturday. The first ten drivers in each went onto Sunday's

The four-year-old Porsche 908/4 of Reinhold Jost and Volkert Merl dominated the Rivet Supply World Championship Six Hour race in August, eventually winning by a clear two laps.

Klaus Ludwig drove this Kremer Racing Porsche 935 to second place with Axel Plankenhorn .

Grand Prix star Riccardo Patrese shared this Lancia Beta Monte Carlo Turbo with rally driver Walter Rohl. The pair finished in fifth place despite overheating problems.

Martin Raymond and his co-driver Tony Charnell were highly impressive in their Chevron B36, the pair finishing third overall and winning the 2 litre class.

ten-lap quarter finals, and the first ten from each of those went into the twelve-lap semis. Ten from each semi then contested the fifteen-lap final. The rain-soaked event was won by Donald MacLeod, who had also been victorious at the very first festival in 1973, held at Snetterton.

And so the seventies came to a close with Brands still the busiest circuit in the country, and still very much a major international venue, loved and respected by drivers and spectators alike.

Not an August Bank Holiday to remember for Nick Foy, whose Formula Ford 2000 Reynard SF79 has crashed.

'Flame out' from a Porsche 935 as it rounds Druids.

Motor Racing at Brands Hatch in the seventies

Then, as now, the Saloon Cars provided close spectacular racing. Eventual winner Brian Muir leads Gordon Spice and Stuart Graham, all in Ford Capri Mk IIIs.

Late in the day and Capris, jostle for position at Paddock Bend. Another season at Brands Hatch draws to a close as the seventies come to an end.

Index